Contents

Kinchaku Drawstring Bag

These pretty drawstring bags are called *kinchaku*, a word derived from *kin* (width) and *chaku* (to wear). In Japan, they are used as kimono accessories and are popular items for decorating with sashiko.

YOU WILL NEED

Two pieces of plain sashiko fabric 11in x 8½in (27.9cm x 21.6cm)

Two pieces of plain cotton 11in x 8½in (27.9cm x 21.5cm) for lining

Two pieces of plain cotton 3½in (8.9cm) square for flower trims

Fine sashiko thread in white and variegated perle thread No 8

Two 25in (63.5cm) lengths of cord for drawstring

FINISHED SIZE:
10½in x 8in (26.7cm x 20.3cm)

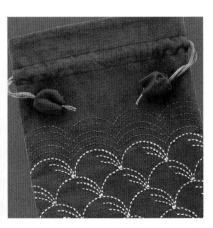

Directions

Marking and stitching the sashiko

1 Mark and cut curved bottom corners on the outside panels and the lining using a 2½in (6.4cm) diameter circle template. Mark and stitch the *nowaki* (grasses) sashiko pattern – see Sashiko Patterns.

Making the bag

2 Assemble the bag using ¼in (6mm) seams throughout. With right sides together, sew one outside panel to one lining piece across the top only. Press the seam towards the outside panel. Repeat with the second panel and lining piece but this time press the seam towards the lining.

3 With right sides together, outer against outer and lining against lining, sew the bag together (Fig 1). Sew to 1in (2.5cm) below the top of the bag. Leave ¾in (1.9cm) gaps unsewn for the drawstring and a 3in (7.6cm) gap unsewn in the lining. Press seams open and clip seam allowances to ⅛in (3mm) around corner curves.

4 Turn right side out, through the lining gap. Push the lining down inside the bag and press. Mark two lines across the bag, joining the ends of the gaps left for the drawstring, 1in (2.5cm) and 1¾in (4.4cm) from the top edge. Stitch around the bag on each line to make a channel. Insert each drawstring, knot the ends and stitch the lining gap closed.

Fig 1

3in (7.6cm) gap

¼in (1.9cm) gaps

Making the flower trim decorations

5 Fold one 3½in (8.9cm) square of cotton in half, right sides together, and sew a ¼in (6mm) seam to make a tube. Turn half of the tube right side out, so the fabric is doubled and seam allowance hidden. Sew running stitches around the raw end of the tube. Slip the tube over the knotted end of the drawstring and gather up tightly (Fig 2). Stitch through the cord and knot to finish off. Fold the tube down over the knot. Sew 'stamens' using yellow thread. Pinch the open end of the tube to flatten it, stitch thread through at the creases and leave loose. Pinch the end the other way and stitch another thread through. Hold all four ends of thread and knot together close to the end of the tube. Trim thread ends.

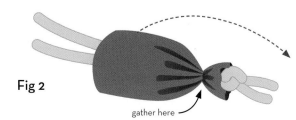

Fig 2

gather here

Shimacho Quilt

The Japanese word 'shimacho' means 'stripe book', which were collections of fabric inspirations. This quilt was inspired by Japanese-style fabrics and makes good use of fabric scraps.

YOU WILL NEED

ASSORTED FEATURE FABRICS:

A – fifty-four 2½in (6.4cm) squares
B – eighteen 4½in (11.4cm) squares
C – nine 6½in (16.5cm) squares
D – twenty-seven strips 4½in x 2½in (11.4cm x 6.4cm)
E – eighteen strips 6½in x 4½in (16.5cm x 11.4cm)
F – nine strips 8½in x 6½in (21.6cm x 16.5cm)
G – nine strips 10½in x 6½in (26.7cm x 16.5cm)

Border fabric 3½yd (3.25m)

Sewing and quilting threads to tone with patchwork

Backing fabric about 76in (193cm) square

Wadding (batting) about 76in (193cm) square

Binding fabric to match border strips about 290in (736.6cm) long

FINISHED SIZE:

68in (172.7cm) square approximately

Directions

Cutting the fabric

1 There are so many strips needed to border the feature fabric patches that it is easier to cut several sets at a time rather than cutting all of them at once, when it is very easy to lose count and either cut too few or too many. The border strips can be sorted into piles with the relevant centre fabrics as you cut. Begin by cutting twenty or so 1½in (3.8cm) strips across the width of the border fabric.

Cut eighteen 9½in (24.1cm) and 11½in (29.2cm) strips and thirty-six 7½in (19cm) strips.

Each 10½in x 6½in (26.7cm x 16.5cm) piece needs two 11½in (29.2cm) and two 7½in (19cm) border strips.

Each 8½in x 6½in (21.6cm x 16.5cm) piece needs two 9½in (24.1cm) and two 7½in (19cm) border strips. The shorter pieces left over from cutting the longer pieces can be used when you cut the borders for the 2½in (6.4cm) squares.

Tip

Although this is a fairly easy quilt to make, there are 144 feature fabric pieces and 576 border pieces (four for each feature fabric patch)! It is not as quick to make as some other quilts, so allow yourself plenty of time to piece it.

2 Continue cutting strips for the medium-sized rectangular patches. Cut thirty-six 7½in (19cm) strips, fifty-four 3½in (8.9cm) strips and ninety 5½in (14cm) strips.

Each 6½in x 4½in (16.5cm x 11.4cm) piece needs two 7½in (19cm) and two 5½in (14cm) border strips.

Each 4½in x 2½in (11.4cm x 6.4cm) piece needs two 5½in (14cm) and two 3½in (8.9cm) strips.

3 Cut the border strips for the squares. Cut thirty-six 7½in (19cm) strips for the 6½in (16.5cm) square borders, seventy-two 5½in (14cm) strips for the 4½in (11.4cm) squares and 216 strips 3½in (8.9cm) long for the 2½in (6.4cm) squares. Keep the remaining fabric to make the long borders on the outside of the quilt.

Sewing the patchwork blocks

4 Using ¼in (6mm) seams throughout, arrange and machine sew the blocks with the 6½in (16.5cm) square patches first. Begin by making a partly sewn seam by stitching the first strip to the centre square but stopping after about 1½in (3.8cm) (indicated by the red line in Fig 1A). Press the seam outwards. Machine sew the next strip to the side of the block. Continue adding strips until the block is complete, then finish the first seam, overlapping the stitches by about ½in (1.3cm).

Fig 1

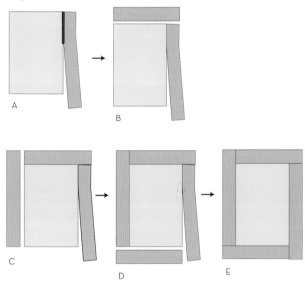

Tip

If you have not sewn a block with part-sewn seams before, begin with one of the larger, square blocks and work your way down to the smaller squares, where the seams are shorter and the space to fit the sewing machine foot into the patchwork seam is slightly less.

5 Machine sew the other blocks with square centre patches, then sew the blocks with the rectangular centre patches. You will need to check that you are sewing the longer border strip side to the longest side of the patch each time – it is easy to get mixed up and sew a short border piece to the longer patch side. Once all the block borders are added, you can arrange and assemble the larger blocks.

6 Lay out the all the pieces for each of the larger blocks as shown in Fig 2. Each 22in (55.9cm) square block is comprised of the following smaller units (shown within the dotted boxes on the diagram). These are, listed by block centre patch size – six A 2½in (6.4cm) squares, two B 4½in (11.4cm) squares, one C 6½in (16.5cm) square, three D 4½in x 2½in (11.4cm x 6.4cm) units, two E 6½in x 4½in (16.5cm x 11.4cm) units, one F 8½in x 6½in (21.6cm x 16.5cm) unit and one G 10½in x 6½in (26.7cm x 16.5cm) unit.

Fig 2

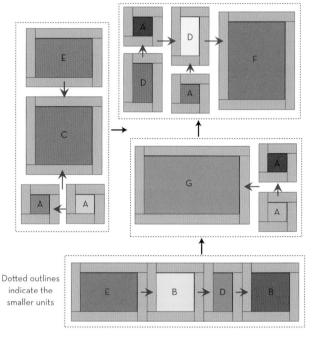

Dotted outlines indicate the smaller units

7 Machine sew the smaller units together to make the larger ones. Begin by sewing the 2½in (6.4cm) centre blocks together. Press seams in the directions indicated by the red arrows on Fig 2, so the seam allowances in adjacent blocks (in the few places where they meet) will lie in opposite directions, enabling the seams to butt up together snugly. The finished large block should look like Fig 3.

Fig 3

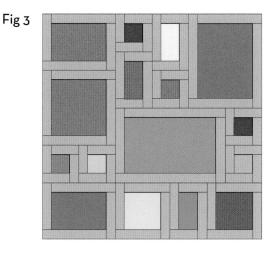

Assembling the quilt top

8 All nine larger blocks are identical, but alternate blocks are turned upside down to create the finished quilt pattern. Lay out the large blocks as shown in Fig 4. The blocks in the corners and the centre of the quilt stay the right way up but turn the other four upside down, achieving the quilt's random look. Machine sew the blocks into columns, pressing the joining seams in opposite directions, and then sew the columns together to make the quilt centre.

9 To add the border, measure your quilt, vertically and horizontally before cutting 1½in (3.8cm) wide fabric strips across the fabric width for the narrow border. The quilt border pieces are added using the same part-sewn seam method as the smaller block borders. For this quilt, these measured 67½in (171.4cm) i.e., the length of one side of the patchwork plus 1in (2.5cm) overlap at the corners. Two strips will need to be joined for each border. If you prefer, sew on each border and trim to length after sewing; for a single narrow border this should not make the quilt edge wavy as it would for multiple borders. Press seams towards the border. Layer and tack (baste) the quilt ready for quilting, if quilting by hand or domestic machine.

Quilting and finishing

10 Free-hand long-arm quilting allows the quilter to follow the asymmetrical piecing with the quilting design, so the feature fabrics appear a little more three-dimensional in the quilting. A meandering design in the borders helps to emphasize the feature fabrics and disguises the seams between the patches, focusing the viewer's attention on all the lovely prints. If you want to make more of a feature of the block borders, try using different shades of the same colour on adjacent blocks, such as mixing dark indigo blues and perhaps quilting along the centre of each strip or in the ditch around the block centres to emphasize the border strips.

11 Bind your quilt to finish. If you use the same fabric for the block borders and binding, it will be almost invisible.

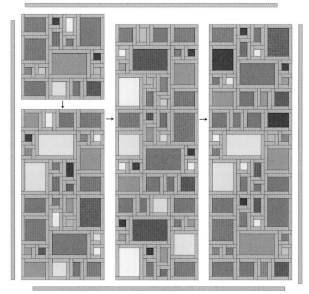

Fig 4

Zabuton Floor Cushion

Zabuton cushions are a feature of traditional Japanese interiors and this large, comfortable cushion is ideal for sitting on. It is made from one Shimacho block – see the Shimacho Quilt.

YOU WILL NEED

One patchwork panel for cushion front

Plain calico (muslin) for backing, larger than the patchwork

Wadding (batting), larger than the patchwork

Fabric for cushion back, same size as quilted and trimmed cushion front plus one zipper with closed end, about 2in (5cm) shorter than cushion side **or** two pieces of fabric for an envelope back (see Tip below)

Three flat buttons if using an envelope back (optional)

Cushion pad to fit cover

FINISHED SIZE:
24in (61cm) square

Directions

Cutting the fabrics

1 To make one Shimacho block as in Fig 1, cut the following from assorted feature fabrics:

A – six 2½in (6.4cm) squares,
B – two 4½in (11.4cm) squares,
C – one 6½in (16.5cm) square,
D – three 4½in x 2½in (11.4cm x 6.4cm) strips,
E – two 6½in x 4½in (16.5cm x 11.4cm) strips,
F – one 10½in x 6½in (26.7cm x 16.5cm) strip,
G – one 8½in x 6½in (21.6cm x 16.5cm) strip.

2 You will also need fabric to border all the fabric pieces – 14in x 43in–44in (35.6cm x 109.2cm–111.8cm) in total. Cut this into nine 1½in (3.8cm) strips across the width of the fabric. Sub-cut the following strips: two 11½in (29.2cm); two 9½in (24.1cm); twelve 7½in (19cm); eighteen 5½in (14cm) and thirty 3½in (8.9cm).

Tip

For an envelope back the two backing panels must overlap enough to avoid the back gaping when in use, but not so much that it is difficult to insert the pad. Cut each panel the same length as the side of the finished cushion panel, but only three-fifths of the width. For example, suitable back panels for a 24in (61cm) square finished cushion would be 24½in x 14½in (62.2cm x 36.8cm).

Making the block

3 The block is made in the same way as the Shimacho Quilt. Lay out the all the pieces for the block as shown in Fig 1. The block is comprised of the following smaller units (shown within the dotted boxes on the diagram). These are, listed by block centre patch size – six A 2½in (6.4cm) squares, two B 4½in (11.4cm) squares, one C 6½in (16.5cm) square, three D 4½in x 2½in (11.4cm x 6.4cm) units, two E 6½in x 4½in (16.5cm x 11.4cm) units, one F 8½in x 6½in (21.6cm x 16.5cm) unit and one G 10½in x 6½in (26.7cm x 16.5cm) unit.

4 Using ¼in (6mm) seams throughout, arrange and machine sew the units for the block beginning with the 6½in (16.5cm) square patch (see Fig 1). Begin by making a partly sewn seam by stitching the first strip to the centre piece but stopping after about 1½in (3.8cm) – see Shimacho Quilt, step 4 Fig 1. Press the seam outwards. Machine sew the next strip to the side of the block. Continue adding strips until the unit is complete, then finish the first seam, overlapping the stitches by ½in (1.3cm).

Fig 1

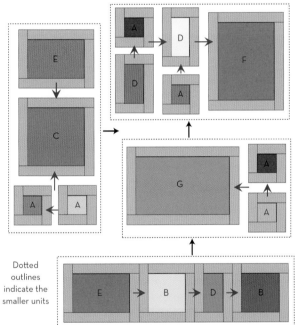

Dotted outlines indicate the smaller units

5 Machine sew the other units with square centre patches, then sew the units with the rectangular centre patches. You will need to check that you are sewing the longer border strip side to the longest side of the patch each time – it is easy to get mixed up and sew a short border piece to the longer patch side. Once all the unit borders are added, you can arrange and assemble the larger units.

6 Machine sew the smaller units together to make the larger ones. Begin by sewing the 2½in (6.4cm) centre blocks together. Press seams in the directions indicated by the red arrows so the seam allowances in adjacent blocks (in the few places where they meet) will lie in opposite directions, enabling the patchwork seams to butt up together snugly. The finished large block should look like Fig 2.

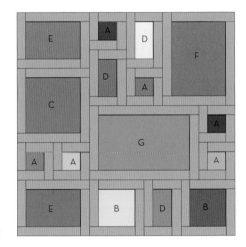

Fig 2

Quilting the cushion panel

7 Layer and tack (baste) the panel ready for quilting, if quilting by hand or domestic machine. Quilt the patchwork pieces in the ditch around the seam lines and add a few extra meandering lines of quilting in the larger pieces. The borders can be quilted with a decorative stitch or left unquilted. The cushion can be finished with a zip closure or an envelope back. Trim the sandwich and then zigzag or overlock the edges of the panel before assembling the cushion. Decide which method you prefer and use the relevant instructions that follow.

Assembling with a zip closure

8 Place the patchwork and cushion backing panel right sides together. Use ½in (1.3cm) seams throughout assembly. With right sides together, machine or hand tack (baste) across the bottom edge (see dashed red line in Fig 3). Machine sew 1in (2.5cm) at the beginning and end of the tacking, starting and finishing with a few backstitches, as shown by the blue line.

Fig 3

9 Press the seam open. From the wrong side, tack the zip in place (make sure the zip pull is facing the right way to open your cushion from the outside!). With the zip foot on the sewing machine, sew the zip in place (see dashed black lines in Fig 4). Check the zip opens properly and remove tacking (basting).

Fig 4

10 With the zip open, place the other three edges of the panel and backing together, pin, and machine sew all round with a ½in (1.3cm) seam allowance. Clip corners, turn right side out through the zip opening, press the seam and insert the pad.

Assembling with an envelope back
11 Hem one long edge of each cushion backing panel by turning over a doubled ¼in (6mm) hem and zigzag or overlock the other edges. Place the patchwork and one of the backing pieces right sides together and pin, as shown in Fig 5.

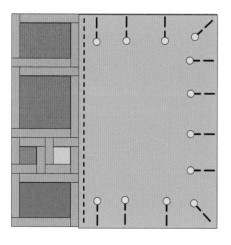

Fig 5

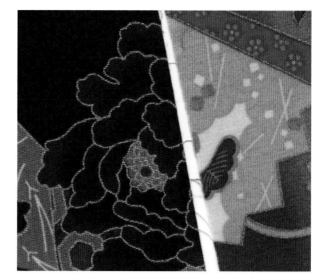

12 Place the second backing piece right sides together, overlapping the first piece, and pin. Machine sew around the edge, with a ½in (1.3cm) seam allowance, as shown by the dashed line in Fig 6. Clip the corners and turn right sides out. Insert the cushion pad through the gap.

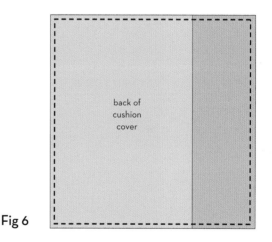

back of cushion cover

Fig 6

Tip
On the envelope back, if the panel overlap will be less than 2in (5cm), add an optional button fastening to the panel edges, working the buttonholes (by hand or machine) on the first backing panel before sewing the panels in place and adding the buttons when the cushion cover is complete. Choose flat buttons so they don't catch so easily on furniture or carpets.

Sashiko Samplers

Small samplers are a good way to practise sashiko patterns and ready-made picture frames display them most elegantly. See Sashiko Patterns for how to stitch the patterns.

YOU WILL NEED

Small picture frame 10in x 4in (25.4cm x 10.2cm)

Self-adhesive mounting card, same size as frame backing board

Sashiko fabric at least ½in (1.3cm) larger than frame size all round

Fine sashiko thread

FINISHED SIZE:

10in x 4in (25.4cm x 10.2cm)

Tip

Commercial frame sizes normally refer to the size of the backing board or image rather than the measurement outside the moulding, so the visible image area will be up to ¼in (6mm) smaller all round.

Directions

Marking and stitching the sashiko

1 Remove any glass in the frame and store carefully. Use the inside of the frame aperture to mark the working area on your fabric. The patterns used are shown here (from left to right): *asanoha* (hemp leaf), *fundō* (scale weights) and *jūji kikkō* (cross tortoiseshell) – see Sashiko Patterns for instructions. Mark the sashiko design on the fabric and then stitch the design.

Framing the samplers

2 Lightly press the work from the back. Arrange the sashiko on the self-adhesive mounting card, make sure the fabric grain is straight and then press into place.

3 Replace the glass in the frame and put the sashiko panel behind it. Replace any necessary packing in the back of the frame and fasten the grips in place.

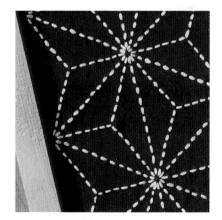

Sensu Quilt

In Japanese 'sensu' means 'fan' and this quilt uses the fan shape in a most creative way.

YOU WILL NEED

FOR THE FAN BLOCKS:

sixteen 8½in (21.6cm) squares for backgrounds and sixteen assorted pieces at least 9½in x 5in (24.1cm x 12.7cm) for fans

Three 64½in (163.8cm) strips of *yukata* cotton, each 14in–15in (35.5cm–38.1cm) wide

or one 64½in (163.8cm) length of patchwork cotton, cut into three 14in (35.5cm) wide strips

Freezer paper to make appliqué templates (on a roll type)

Sewing thread to tone with patchwork and quilting thread to contrast

Backing fabric slightly larger than finished quilt top

Wadding (batting) slightly larger than finished quilt top

Binding fabric 260in (660cm) length

FINISHED SIZE:

64in (162.5cm) long x up to 58in (147.3cm) wide (with *yukata*/kimono fabric)

Directions

Cutting the fabric

1 Trace off sixteen freezer paper fan outlines from the fan template (Fig 1). Using the iron on a cool setting, iron each template on to the back of a piece of the fan fabric, arranging the fans so that attractive motifs are framed by the fans. Cut out the fans, allowing a generous ¼in-⅜in (6mm-1cm) hem allowance on the curves but none along the straight sides, as shown in Fig 2. The seam allowances on the straight sides are included in the template and the dashed lines show where the ends of the fan will be sewn into the patchwork seams.

Making the appliqué

2 Press the hem allowance over the curved edge of the freezer paper fan with the iron on a slightly higher temperature, but being careful not to scorch your fabrics and only pressing the very edge. You will need to clip the fabric around the inside of the smaller curve, cutting almost up to the freezer paper but not quite. Allow the pieces to cool.

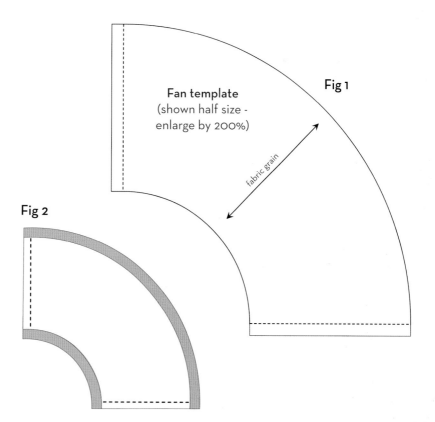

Fan template (shown half size - enlarge by 200%)

fabric grain

Fig 1

Fig 2

15

3 Pin one fan to the centre backing square, so the freezer paper is sandwiched between the appliqué fan and the backing square, with the raw edges all tucked under the curved edges, arranging the pins along the inner and outer curves as shown in Fig 3. When it is correctly positioned the straight edges at each end of the fan will be touching the edges of the square.

Fig 3

Tip

Half the fan blocks will be rotated by 90 degrees, so think carefully if using a directional fabric for the background or a stripe as it will be on its side in half the blocks. If the background fabric is abstract with diagonal bands, this can make an interesting zigzag effect. If using a landscape print, it would need to be the right way up in each block.

4 The appliqué can be hand or machine sewn to the backing square. Do not sew across the straight ends of the fans. Turn each block over and carefully cut away the background fabric, leaving a generous ¼in (6mm) allowance behind each fan. Remove the freezer paper by peeling it away from the back of the fans. Gently scrunching up the paper along the fan edges will help loosen it from the appliqué stitches. Appliqué fans to all sixteen blocks.

Making the patchwork

5 Lay out the fan blocks into two columns of eight blocks each, turning half the blocks through 90 degrees, as shown in Fig 4. The placement of the different fans is very much a matter of personal taste and a random arrangement works best. Once you are happy with the block layout, machine sew them together in pairs using a ¼in (6mm) seam allowance and sew the pairs together to make two columns of eight blocks each. Press the seams downwards.

Fig 4

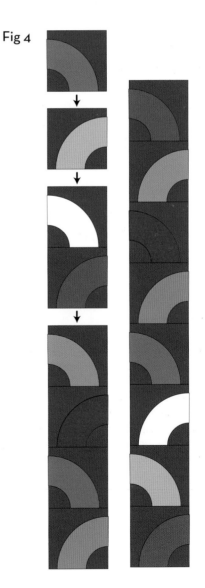

Assembling the quilt top

6 Arrange the patchwork strips between the three 64½in (163.8cm) long strips (Fig 5). (Note: patchwork fabric 42in–44in (106.7cm–111.7cm) wide can be cut into three 14in (35.5cm) wide strips and used instead of *yukata* cotton, but the finished quilt will be slightly narrower.) The pattern repeat will be in a slightly different position on each long strip, so move the three strips around until you are happy with the sequence. This is particularly important if you have three strips cut from patchwork fabric, as the pattern may look odd if it continues very obviously on either side of the fan patchwork strip. Machine sew the columns together to complete the quilt centre and press vertical seams towards the long strips, away from the patchwork.

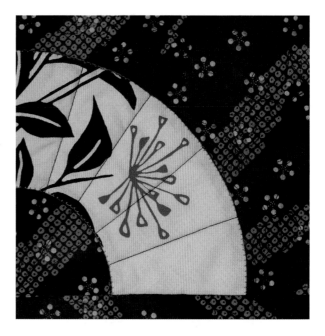

8 Bind your quilt to finish. Select a fabric to coordinate with your quilt, such as dark blue. A slightly darker binding can frame the quilt and also looks better against the ends of the fan block strips.

Tip

If you have some spare fabrics or blocks and would like a hand-guided design for your quilt, ask your quilter if they could use them, as you will be able to get a very good impression of how the quilting will work. Feel free to discuss your ideas with your quilter – a good professional quilter will welcome input.

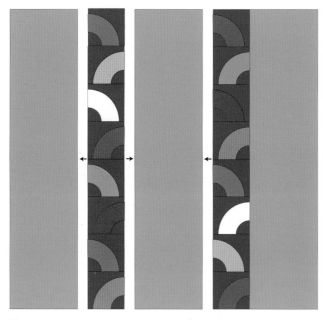

Fig 5

Quilting and finishing

7 Layer and tack (baste) the quilt ready for quilting, if quilting by hand or domestic machine. Free-motion long-arm quilting was chosen for this quilt because the beautiful stencilled vintage *yukata* cotton had a design worth emphasizing, rather than using a pantograph design down each *yukata* strip – an option that would work well with many fabrics. The quilter experimented with ideas on smaller samples and decided to add some extra quilting to the landscape *yukata* cotton, to bring out the shapes of the farmhouses.

Sashiko Tote Bag

The front of a tote bag is a good place to show off a sashiko panel, especially when it is as bright as this one. Using a checked fabric makes stitching the sashiko really easy.

YOU WILL NEED

Checked fabric 12in x 9in (30.5cm x 22.8cm)

Medium weight denim:
two pieces 3½in x 9in (8.9cm x 22.8cm) for top and bottom borders
two pieces 3in x 17in (7.6cm x 43.2cm) for side borders
one piece 13in x 17in (33cm x 43.2cm) for back

Medium sashiko thread in white

Two pieces of orange cotton fabric 13in x 17in (33cm x 43.2cm), for lining

Two 12in (30.5cm) lengths of 1in (2.5cm) wide cotton webbing for straps

Finished size:
12in x 16in (30.5cm x 40.6cm)

Directions

Marking and stitching the sashiko

1 Select and stitch the sashiko pattern, which is a variation of *komezashi* (rice stitch) – see Sashiko Patterns. Lightly press the finished sashiko from the wrong side.

Making up the bag

2 With right sides together, machine sew one 9in x 3½in (22.8cm x 8.9cm) piece of denim to the top of the centre panel, using a ½in (1.3cm) seam. Sew the second piece to the bottom and press both seams outwards. Sew the 17in x 3in (43.2cm x 7.6cm) pieces to either side of the panel. Press seams outwards.

3 Arrange the webbing straps on the right side of the front and back panels as in Fig 1, allowing the strap ends to overlap the panel edge by ½in (1.3cm). The gap between straps ends is 4in (10.2cm). Tack (baste) in place.

4 With the front and back panels right sides together and using a ¼in (6mm) seam, machine sew down the side, across the bottom and up the other side. Clip the corners within the seam allowance but don't cut right up to the stitches. Press the seam to one side.

5 Make the lining by placing the two pieces of orange cotton fabric right sides together and, with a ¼in (6mm) seam, machine sew down the side, across the bottom and up part of the other side (Fig 2). Leave a 4in (10.2cm) gap unsewn and sew the remaining side seam. Press the seam to one side.

6 Turn the outer bag section right side out through the gap. Keeping the bag lining turned inside out, place the bag outer inside the lining, lining up the top edge and side seams. Line up the side seams so they are pressed in alternate directions (Fig 3). Machine sew around the top of the bag, sewing the lining to the bag outer all round with a ¼in (6mm) seam.

7 Turn the bag right side out through the unsewn gap in the lining side seam. Press the seam at the top of the bag. Machine or hand sew around the top of the bag, about ⅛in (3mm) from the edge. Turn the bag inside out and slip stitch the gap closed to finish.

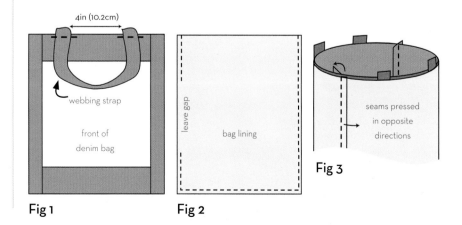

Fig 1

Fig 2

Fig 3

Kimono Quilt

The kimono outline is an instantly recognisable design and this project features that motif in a stunning quilt. Flower-themed prints were used for the kimono appliqués.

YOU WILL NEED

Twelve fat quarters for kimono fabrics

Twelve 12½in (31.8cm) squares of background fabric

Twelve assorted block borders for each block:
two strips 12½in x 1½in (31.8cm x 3.8cm)
two strips 14½in x 1½in (36.8cm x 3.8cm)

Shaded cotton for sashing 41in (104cm) x
width of fabric

FABRIC FOR BORDER:
two strips 66½in x 7½in (168.9cm x 19cm)
two strips 64½in x 7½in (163.8cm x 19cm)

Twelve 12½in (31.8cm) squares of freezer paper

Backing fabric slightly larger than quilt top

Wadding (batting) slightly larger than quilt top

Binding fabric 300in (762cm) length

FINISHED SIZE:
80in x 64in (203.2cm x 162.6cm)

Directions

Making the appliqués

1 Following the measurements in Fig 1, draft a master template for the kimono block or photocopy. Alternatively, enlarge the pattern given here by 400% so it measures 12½in (31.7cm) square. Trace twelve kimono shapes on to the freezer paper and cut out carefully.

Fig 1

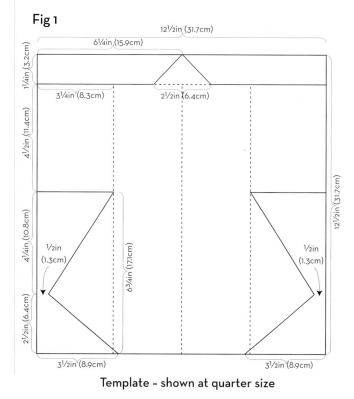

Template – shown at quarter size

2 For each kimono block appliqué, iron the freezer paper template on to the back of each piece of kimono fabric. Cut out the kimono, a generous ¼in (6mm) away from the edge of the paper to allow for the appliqué hem (see Fig 2), except for at the ends of the sleeves and the bottom hem, where a seam allowance is already included. Clip the seam allowance at the points indicated by the arrows. Press the hem allowance over the edge of the freezer paper shapes with the iron, only pressing the very edge. Allow the pieces to cool.

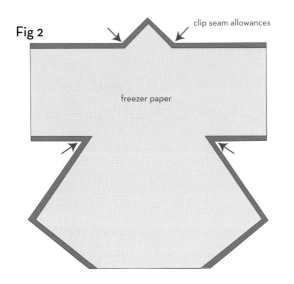

Fig 2

clip seam allowances

freezer paper

3 Pin a kimono to a centre backing square, so the freezer paper is sandwiched between the appliqué and the backing square. Line up the sleeve and hem edges with the square, with raw edges all tucked under, arranging pins as in Fig 3. Add more pins to hold securely in place. Hand or machine sew the appliqué in place. Turn each block over and cut away the background fabric, leaving a generous ¼in (6mm) allowance behind each kimono. Peel the paper away from the back of the kimono. Appliqué kimono to all twelve blocks.

Fig 3

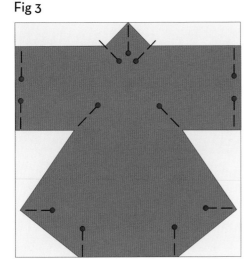

Sewing the block borders

4 Machine sew two 12½in x 1½in (21.8cm x 3.8cm) border strips to the top and bottom of each appliqué block. Sew the two 14½in x 1½in (36.8cm x 3.8cm) strips to the block sides, as Fig 4. Press seams towards the outside of the block each time.

Fig 4

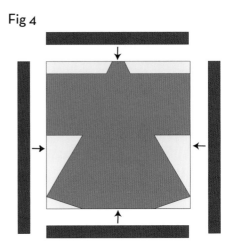

5 Shaded fabric is used for the sashing. Cut sixteen 2½in (6.4cm) wide strips across the fabric width first and then cut eleven 30½in (77.5cm) long sashing strips from the strip centres and nine 16½in (41.9cm) sashing strips from either end.

Assembling the quilt top

6 Lay out the blocks as in Fig 5, in the order you wish. Position the sashing strips in the correct places, turning the strips around to obtain the shading effect. Start assembling the quilt top using a part-sewn seam method (see Shimacho Quilt, step 4, Fig 1). Machine sew the sashing to the blocks, starting with

the seams indicated by the blue lines in Fig 6, sewing only about 2in (5cm) of each seam. Continue joining the blocks and sashing along the seams indicated by the yellow lines, also sewing only about 2in (5cm) until all the blocks and sashing strips are joined at the beginning and end of each strip. Finger press seam allowances towards the sashing strips. Working your way across the patchwork, return to each partly sewn seam and complete sewing the centre section of each seam, overlapping the previous stitches by about ½in (1.3cm). Press seams towards the sashing.

Fig 5

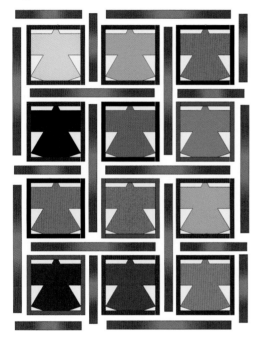

Fig 6

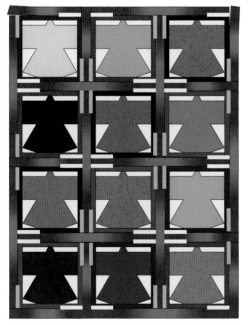

7 Add the border by first measuring your quilt top and cut fabric strips for the borders. Sew the 66½in x 7½in (168.9cm x 19cm) long quilt borders to either side first, and then add the shorter border strips across the top and bottom (Fig 7). Press seams towards the quilt border. Layer and tack (baste) the quilt ready for quilting, if quilting by hand or domestic machine.

Fig 7

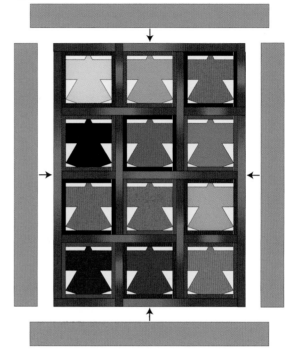

Quilting and finishing

8 This quilt was free-hand quilted on a long-arm machine, with each kimono block treated individually. The little kimono lend themselves to being quilted to imitate real life kimono seams, with vertical lines up the centre back and down from each shoulder, as indicated by the dashed lines in Fig 1, which could be done with a walking foot on a domestic sewing machine or be hand quilted.

9 Bind your quilt to finish – a slightly darker blue binding will help to frame the quilt.

Moyōzashi Table Runner

A table runner is a good project for a sashiko sampler. The five patterns used here were (top to bottom): *Kawari asanoha, ganzezashi* and variation, *yatsude asanoha* and *shippō tsunagi*. See Sashiko Patterns for how to stitch the patterns.

YOU WILL NEED

Sashiko fabric 34½in x 7in (87.6cm x 17.8cm)

Striped *tsumugi* cotton:
two pieces 34½in x 5in (87.6cm x 12.7cm)
two pieces 5in x 15in (12.7cm x 38.1cm)

Butter muslin 43in x 15in (109cm x 38.1cm)

Plain black cotton 42½in x 15in (108cm x 38.1cm) for backing

Fine sashiko thread in various colours

FINISHED SIZE:

41in x 13½in (104cm x 34.3cm)

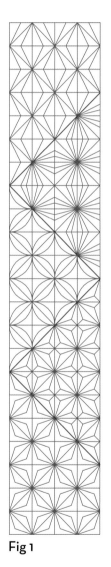

Fig 1

Directions

Marking and stitching the sashiko

1 All the patterns on this runner were based on a 1½in (3.8cm) grid and the full design is shown in Fig 1 (see also Sashiko Patterns). Zigzag the edges of the sashiko fabric to prevent fraying, then mark the patterns and stitch the sashiko. Lightly press the finished sashiko from the wrong side.

Assembling the central panel

2 With right sides together, machine sew one 34½in x 5in (87.6cm x 12.7cm) piece of striped cotton to the side of the sashiko panel, using a ½in (1.3cm) seam. Sew the second piece to the opposite side. Press seams outwards. Machine sew the 5in x 15in (12.7cm x 38.1cm) pieces of cotton to either side of the central panel. Press seams outwards. Tack (baste) the muslin to the back of the panel and then stitch the lines of sashiko in the border through both layers.

Making up the runner

3 Place the front panel and backing fabric right sides together and pin all round. Machine sew with a ½in (1.3cm) seam allowance, leaving an 8in (20.3cm) gap at the centre of the lower edge. Trim off the corners within the seam allowance, but do not cut right up to the stitches. Turn the runner right way out through the unsewn gap. Ease the corners out so they are nice and sharp. Lay the runner flat and smooth it out. Turn under the raw edges at the bottom, pin or tack (baste) and slip stitch the gap closed. From the back, sew around the whole panel ¼in (6mm) from the edge with small hand stitches through the backing and seam allowances only, to keep the backing in place.

Sashiko Herb Pillow

Woven checks and stripes making stitching some sashiko patterns really easy. The pattern used here is called *kawari dan tsunagi* (linked steps variation), shown below.

YOU WILL NEED

Checked cotton fabric
19in x 11in (48.3cm x 27.9cm)

Plain calico 19in x 11in
(48.3cm x 27.9cm)

Scraps of fabric and wadding
(batting) to stuff pillow

Sewing thread and fine sashiko
thread in cream

Herbs and/or essential oils
(aromatherapy oils)

FINISHED SIZE:

9¼in x 10½in (23.5cm x 26.7cm)

Directions

Stitching the sashiko

1 Take the checked cotton fabric and fold it in half to 9½in x 11in (24.1cm x 27.9cm) to find the centre line. If the checks are ⅝in (1.6cm) and the piece is centred on the pattern, the fold will be along the centre of a row of checks, not on the edge. Begin stitching along the edge of a row of checks, one and a half rows from the fold line (see Fig 1). Three whole squares from the end of the line, turn the stitching through 90 degrees and stitch across three squares and then turn again and stitch back along the next row. Continue until the first half of the panel is stitched, then complete the second half. Press each finished square.

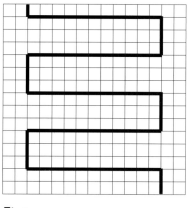

Fig 1

If the checks are not ⅝in (1.6cm) you could change the number of check squares from the end of each row and the number of squares in between rows. The smaller the spacing between stitch rows, the more stitching you will have to do overall.

Making the pillow pad

2 Fold the calico in half, right sides together, to 9½in x 11in (24.1cm x 27.9cm). Machine sew down each side and across the bottom edge with a ¼in (6mm) seam allowance, leaving a 4in (10.2cm) gap. Start and finish each seam with a few backstitches.

3 Turn the pad right side out through the gap and make sure the corners are well turned out. Stuff with the fabric and wadding (batting) scraps, mixing in herbs and a few drops of essential oil. Slip stitch the gap closed with small stitches so the filling can't escape.

Making the pillow cover

4 Fold the sashiko panel in half, and machine sew with a ¼in (6mm) seam allowance, as for the pillow pad above, but leaving an 8in (20.3cm) gap unsewn across the bottom edge. Press and make sure the corners are well turned out. Ease the cover over the pillow pad. Pin and slip stitch the gap closed.

Koshi Sofa Throw

This sofa throw is really easy to make, especially with striped fabrics. The pattern used was *kawari dan tsunagi* (linked steps variation) – see the Sashiko Herb Pillow, Fig 1.

YOU WILL NEED

Striped cotton 52⅛in x 10½in (132.4cm x 26.7cm)

Striped cotton 52⅛in x 10½in (132.4cm x 26cm)

CHECKED COTTON A:

two outer strips 50¼in x 11¼in (127.6cm x 28.6cm)

one centre strip 50¼in x 10⅞in (127.6cm x 27.6cm)

CHECKED COTTON B:

two strips 50¼in x 10⅞in (127.6cm x 27.6cm)

Backing fabric 69½in x 52⅛in (176.5cm x 132.4cm)

Sewing thread to match fabrics and fine cream sashiko thread

FINISHED SIZE:

68in x 51⅜in (172.7cm x 130.5cm)

Tip

The size of the checks and stripe used are ⅜in (1cm), so it was easiest to cut them for a ⅜in (1cm) seam allowance. Cut along the checks and stripe with scissors for accurate lines.

Directions

Sewing the patchwork

1 Cut along the nearest woven line in the check or stripe pattern each time. If your fabric has a different check size, you could resize the pieces to suit your fabric better. For example, if it is a ½in (1.3cm) check, panel widths and lengths to the nearest ½in will work better.

2 Pin in pairs, right sides together (Fig 1), lining up checks and sew with a ⅜in (1cm) seam. Press seams to one side. Sew all five strips together.

3 Pin striped panels on each end, lining up stripe with check and sew together. Press seams towards the striped fabric. Assemble the backing panel and press any seams open to reduce bulk.

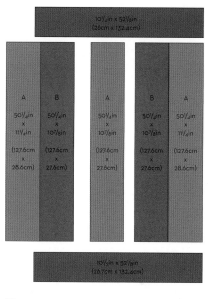

Fig 1

Layering and hemming

4 Pin the patchwork to the backing fabric, wrong sides together. Tack (baste) together, about ½in (1.3cm) from seam lines and at intervals of about 3in (7.6cm) down and across the throw. Tack all around 1in (2.5cm) from the edge.

5 Turn under the patchwork edge ⅜in (1cm) and tack ⅛in (3mm) from the folded edge. Turn over and repeat with the backing, turning the edge under to match the patchwork edge and tacking the backing fabric to the front as you turn it. Slip stitch all round, stitching the backing to the top. Remove tacking.

6 Stitch a single sashiko line all around the throw. Quilt in the seam ditch, using thread to tone with the fabrics rather than the sashiko thread.

Stitching the sashiko

7 Fold the throw in half to find the middle of the check strips and begin the sashiko from the middle of the centre strip, working along the strip. Each section of the step pattern is seven squares wide, about 2⅝in (6.7cm), and the stitch line turns through 90 degrees three squares from the edge of each strip. Pull the knotted thread between the layers at the beginning and end of stitching. To finish, stitch plain rows along the striped fabrics at the top and bottom, six stripes apart.

Sashiko Patterns

The sashiko patterns used on the projects in this book are shown here, with stitching instructions and diagrams.

 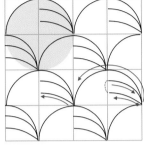

Nowaki (grasses)

Used on the Kinchaku Drawstring Bag. Mark a grid – the sample is 1in. Use a 2in diameter circle template to mark the arcs. Use the same template to mark the curved grasses. Stitch across the row, following the red arrows. Stitch the lower grass first, strand loosely across back to stitch the upper grass and finally stitch across the arc. Repeat to the end of the row.

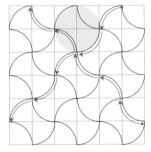 

Fundō (scale weights)

Used on the Sashiko Samplers. This pattern is half of *shippō tsunagi* – only one wavy line is stitched on each diagonal. Mark a grid – the sample is 1in. Use a 2in circle template (shown in blue) to mark wavy lines. Following the red arrows, stitch diagonal wavy lines (shown as red and light brown).

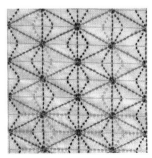 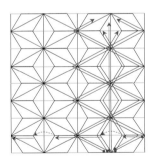

Asanoha (hemp leaf)

Used on the Sashiko Samplers. Mark a grid – the sample is 1½in. Divide squares horizontally into rectangles. Use the grid as a guide to mark the large zigzag lines. Don't mark the shallow vertical zigzags until after you have stitched the main vertical lines and the large zigzag lines. Don't let your stitches cross on the front where pattern lines intersect. Following the red arrows, stitch the vertical lines (shown in red on the stitched sample). Then stitch the diagonal lines as zigzags, forming figures of eight (shown in light brown and yellow). Mark and stitch shallow vertical zigzags, also as figures of eight (dark brown and dark green). Stitch the short horizontal lines (turquoise), keeping thread continuous and stranding across the back (red dashed lines on diagram).

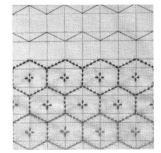 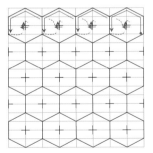

Jūji kikkō (cross tortoiseshell)

Used on the Sashiko Samplers. Mark a grid – the sample is ⅜in x ¾in. Mark diagonal lines to form the tops of the hexagons. Following the red arrows, stitch the pattern in rows, stitching around three sides of the hexagon (shown in red on the stitched sample), keeping the thread continuous and stranding across the back to stitch the centre crosses (indicated by red dashed lines in the diagram).

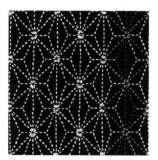 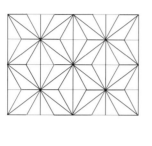

KAWARI ASANOHA (HEMP LEAF VARIATION)

Used on the Moyōzashi Table Runner. This is a distorted version of the asanoha pattern. Mark a grid – the sample is 1in. Do not divide the grid further before marking the pattern. Continue to mark and stitch, following the instructions for *asanoha*.

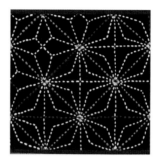 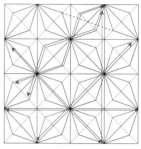

GANZEZASHI (SEA URCHIN STITCH)

Used on the Moyōzashi Table Runner. Mark a grid – the sample is 1½in. Mark diagonal lines. Mark the zigzag lines using the dashed line in the diagram as a guide. Following the red arrows, stitch vertical lines (shown in red on the stitched sample). Stitch horizontal lines (shown in light brown) and then the diagonal lines (yellow and light green). Work the zigzags in a continuous line (dark brown and dark green).

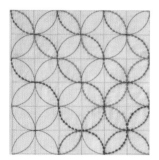 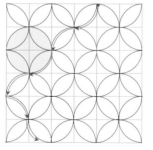

SHIPPŌ TSUNAGI (LINKED SEVEN TREASURES)

Used on the Mōyozashi Table Runner. Mark a grid – the sample is 1in. Use a 2in circle template to mark the interlocking circles (shown in blue on the diagram). Following the red arrows, stitch diagonal wavy lines (shown in red on the stitched sample). Work around the pattern in a continuous line (shown in light brown and yellow).

 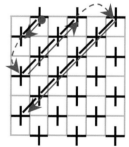

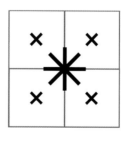

KOMEZASHI (RICE STITCH)

Used on the Sashiko Tote Bag. Start by stitching back and forth across the grid – the bag fabric check was used as the grid for the bag. Stitch the second set of stitches by eye, to cross over the first set at right angles. For the bag, further sets of stitches were worked at 45 degrees, in a star pattern. The diagonal stitching was omitted and cross stitches worked in the centre of the checked squares.

About the Author

SUSAN BRISCOE writes and designs for patchwork and quilting magazines and teaches patchwork and sashiko quilting in the UK and overseas. A graduate of UCW Aberystwyth, she began quilting after working as an Assistant English Teacher on the JET (Japan Exchange Teaching) programme in Yuza-machi, Yamagata Prefecture, Japan, in the early 1990s, where traditional textiles, architecture, landscape, the tea ceremony and local festivals provided inspiration. Specializing in Japanese textile themes, she has written over ten books on quilting, including three books on patchwork bags and two books on Japanese sashiko.

A DAVID & CHARLES BOOK

© F&W Media International, Ltd 2013

David & Charles is an imprint of F&W Media International, Ltd
Brunel House, Forde Close, Newton Abbot, TQ12 4PU, UK

F&W Media International, Ltd is a subsidiary of F+W Media, Inc
10151 Carver Road, Suite #200, Blue Ash, OH 45242, USA

Text and Designs © Susan Briscoe 2013
Layout and Photography © F&W Media International, Ltd 2013

First published in the UK and USA in 2013

A catalogue record for this book is available from the British Library.

ISBN-13: 978-1-4463-0350-4 paperback
ISBN-10: 1-4463-0350-0 paperback

Printed in China by RR Donnelley for
F&W Media International, Ltd
Brunel House, Forde Close, Newton Abbot, TQ12 4PU, UK

10 9 8 7 6 5 4 3 2 1

F+W Media publishes high quality books on a wide range of subjects. For more great book ideas visit: www.stitchcraftcreate.co.uk